Land Research Records

A Family Tree Research Workbook

By Catherine Coulter

Other Books by Catherine Coulter

www.amazon.com/author/cathycoulter

Family Tree Research Workbook a series of 10 books

Census Research Records   My Family Tree Notebook

Military Research Records   Web Log and Web Account

Court House Research Records   Immigration Research Records

Naturalization Research Records

Family Group Research Records

My Family Tree Research Workbook

Cemetery and Funeral Research Records

My Blood Pressure Chart

Journals and Address
Eye of the Tiger
Lion
Whatever
Internet Addresses and Accounts

Children's Books
The Man in Red
A Child's Book of Poems
Little Net Book Blue
Little Net Book Pink
Little Net Book Yellow
Little Net Book Black

Land /Deeds

The land/deed research log in this book will help you at the court house when searching for the land records. It will help keep track of those you have found and those you still want to look for. It also will help you keep track of which county and state you have searched land/deed records for your ancestors. You can use these pages one page per surname if you wish.

The indexes for the land/deed records are most likely are listed under the grantor or grantee's names. The term grantor means the person who is selling the land. The grantee is the person buying the land. You will then have to search them page by page to find your ancestor. You can put the ancestor's name you want to look for in the right column before you go to the court house and then you will have every one you want to search for on hand. I advise putting the names in alphabetical order to make searching easier. You will be able to fill the rest of this information in as you find the records.

Once the log is competed it will also give you a list of sources to use for verifying the records you have found. If you run out of time at the court house and need to go back at a later date to look at the land/deed records you will have all the information you will need already to locate them.

Land /deed records can be useful in searching for information on your ancestors but don't be surprised if you don't always find land records for some. As with today, some of our ancestors did not always own the land they lived on. Some rented land and homes, some were borders and then there were the ancestors who were employees of the people who owned the land. Searching for land/deeds is still worth doing because of the potential information that you may gain.

One piece of information that you will be able find is the date they bought the land. Keep in mind that the date may not be the exact date they moved on to the land. It dose though give you an approximant date that they came to that county. If they were coming from far away the husband of a family would sometimes come by himself to check out the area and buy some land for his family and at a later date they would move there. Sometimes the delay in moving on to the land was because they needed to save up some more money to travel to the newly acquired land and build a home.

The land records usually give the place where they lived at the time they bought the land. This will help document their residency there and possibly give you clues as to where to look for them next. It is always a good idea to check the land records where they had been living at the time of the sale to see if they owned land before. It will give you an idea where they lived before that as well. It establishes a trail for you to follow. Keep in mind that just because they left one place to move somewhere else does not mean they didn't move back to the same area that they left so it makes sense to look completely through the land/deed records and not stop when you find one record.

Another thing to keep in mind is that just because they moved on to a different place does not mean they sold the land they left before they left it or gave it to someone else. It is possible that they sold it later after the move. It then stands to reason that it is a good idea to search for the sale of this land as well as when they bought it.

You can learn how much land they owned and where it's located or a brief description of it. Farmers sometimes would also buy more land around or nearby later on in order to expand the farm. Sometimes their grown children would buy land adjacent to or nearby their parents to raise their own family and farm for themselves. The grown children may even add their land to their parents and thus continue to farm with their parents while expanding the family farm.

The land records will also tell you who sold them the land. Don't be surprised to find a parent or relative either sold or gifted them with land. This could be useful for you as well. It will include the price they paid for the land, if it was not a gift, and how many acres were sold.

One of your ancestors, if they had been in the military during the Revolutionary War or the War of 1812 very well could have received land for their service as a form of payment. In this situation you may find more information about him. You may find not only his residence but information on his enlistment. The information could be as simple as which company or regiment he was in to how long he was enlisted and his rank. If he actually moved on to that land it could be the reason he moved. He may have sold the land or gifted it to someone, just because he received a bounty land does not necessarily mean he kept it or lived on it.

Grantor Index Forms

County Land Records = Grantor

Grantor	Grantee	Book	Vol	Page	Date of Deed	Date of Record	Location

County Land Records = Grantor

Grantor	Grantee	Book	Vol	Page	Date of Deed	Date of Record	Location

County Land Records = Grantor

Grantor	Grantee	Book	Vol	Page	Date of Deed	Date of Record	Location

County Land Records = Grantor

Grantor	Grantee	Book	Vol	Page	Date of Deed	Date of Record	Location

County Land Records = Grantor

Grantor	Grantee	Book	Vol	Page	Date of Deed	Date of Record	Location

County Land Records = Grantor

Grantor	Grantee	Book	Vol	Page	Date of Deed	Date of Record	Location

_____ County Land Records = Grantor

Grantor	Grantee	Book	Vol	Page	Date of Deed	Date of Record	Location

County Land Records = Grantor

Grantor	Grantee	Book	Vol	Page	Date of Deed	Date of Record	Location

_____ County Land Records = Grantor

Grantor	Grantee	Book	Vol	Page	Date of Deed	Date of Record	Location

County Land Records = Grantor

Grantor	Grantee	Book	Vol	Page	Date of Deed	Date of Record	Location

Grantee Index Forms

County Land Records = Grantee

Grantee	Grantor	Book	Vol	Page	Date of Deed	Date of Record	Location

County Land Records = Grantee

Grantee	Grantor	Book	Vol	Page	Date of Deed	Date of Record	Location

_____ County Land Records = Grantee

Grantee	Grantor	Book	Vol	Page	Date of Deed	Date of Record	Location

County Land Records = Grantee

Grantee	Grantor	Book	Vol	Page	Date of Deed	Date of Record	Location

County Land Records = Grantee

Grantee	Grantor	Book	Vol	Page	Date of Deed	Date of Record	Location

County Land Records = Grantee

Grantee	Grantor	Book	Vol	Page	Date of Deed	Date of Record	Location

_____ County Land Records = Grantee

Grantee	Grantor	Book	Vol	Page	Date of Deed	Date of Record	Location

County Land Records = Grantee

Grantee	Grantor	Book	Vol	Page	Date of Deed	Date of Record	Location

County Land Records = Grantee

Grantee	Grantor	Book	Vol	Page	Date of Deed	Date of Record	Location

_____ County Land Records = Grantee

Grantee	Grantor	Book	Vol	Page	Date of Deed	Date of Record	Location

Notes

Notes

Notes

Notes